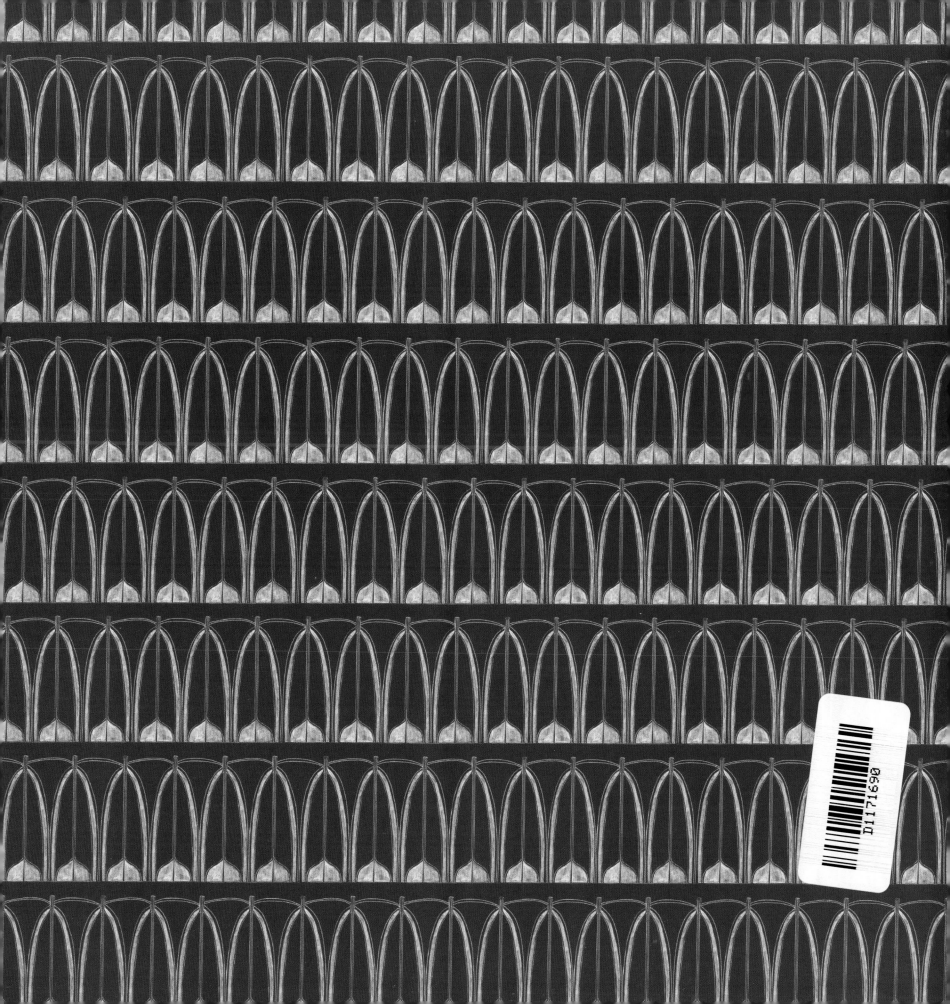

For Ashby!

love

2022

KATIE YAMASAKI

SHAPES, LINES, and LIGHT

My Grandfather's
American Journey

Norton Young Readers • An Imprint of W. W. Norton & Company • Independent Publishers Since 1923

For Pop, Uncle Taro, and in loving memory of Aunty Carol.

Special thanks to Densho.org; and to Justin Beal and Dale Gyure for their support, incredible insight, and devoted research into my grandfather's life and work.

For information about permission to reproduce selections from this book, write to Permissions, W. W. Norton & Company, Inc., 500 Fifth Avenue, New York, NY 10110

For information about special discounts for bulk purchases, please contact W. W. Norton Special Sales at specialsales@wwnorton.com or 800-233-4830

Manufacturing by Toppan Leefung
Book design by Hana Anouk Nakamura
Production manager: Julia Druskin

ISBN 978-1-324-01701-1

W. W. Norton & Company, Inc., 500 Fifth Avenue, New York, N.Y. 10110
www.wwnorton.com
W. W. Norton & Company Ltd., 15 Carlisle Street, London W1D 3BS

0 9 8 7 6 5 4 3 2 1

Old people, it turns out, were not always old.
Not even grandparents.

I learned that about my grandfather, Minoru.
He was an architect and I called him Grandpa.
My grandma called him Tinky. Some people called
him Min, and the world called him Yama.

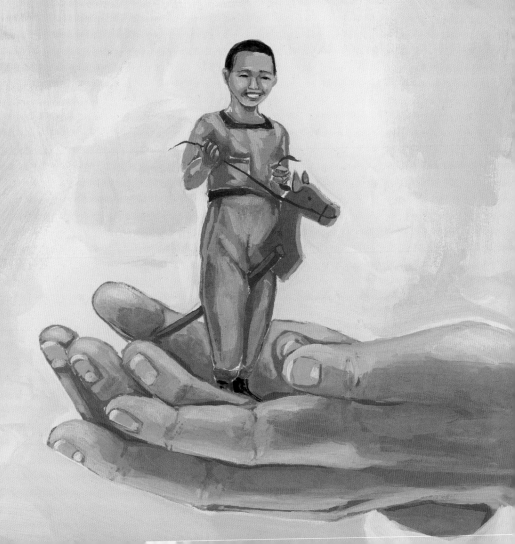

Before he was my grandpa, he was a kid.

A teenager even!

A young man trying to find his way through the world.

A lot of the world happened to him.

And he happened to a lot of the world.

When Yama was young, he noticed a feeling in his chest that changed from space to space. In his rickety home, in his crowded neighborhood, and with his mother, father, and brother, he felt welcome. He felt curious and open. He felt seen.

But there were other spaces.
Buildings that closed the open place in his heart.
Spaces that said, "You are not welcome here.
Not your kind."

"Perhaps you will stock shoes for a store like your father."
But there was a quiet voice inside Yama.
My father is brilliant.

"Perhaps you will sweep factory floors on
weekends like your father."
The quiet voice spoke again.
My father works hard.

"Perhaps architecture is too far a reach
for someone like you."
Yama listened to the quiet voice.
You have no idea how far I can reach.

Yama went instead to spaces where he felt welcome.
Forests deep with evergreen.
Streams that sang him a calming song.
Sunlight glinting off rocks.
Spaces of light and freedom ignited his imagination.

He worked harder than everyone else, swallowing the sharp ache
that came from not being seen. Faces like his in places like this.
He listened to that quiet voice inside.
I will go to college and build my life.

But there was no money.

Only freezing cold, far away, north, way north, Alaska.
Sweeping vistas, glittering waters.

And dark canneries that reeked of rotten fish.
No fresh air. No light.
No rest working eighteen-hour days.
So many Nisei like him—those born in America
to parents who had come from Japan.
Is this where they think we belong?

I am building. I am saving.

Every summer, Yama went to Alaska
and paid his way through college.

Yama studied for many years. He stayed at the top of his class.
Beautiful drawings, ideas like gardens growing in his mind. . . .
He was something special.

But when it was time to get a job,
America was in the middle of
the Great Depression.
Doors slammed. Not hiring.

Especially—
Eyes like yours.
Names like yours.
Faces like yours.

And when he did get a job,
designing buildings, the world still told him,
"We do not trust your Japanese name.
Your Japanese face."
Have you ever tasted something bitter in your mouth?
That's how they said "Japanese."

He kept working. Harder than anyone else.
He married a pianist named Teruko.
The soulful sound of her music found its way into his work.

Just after they wed, war began.
Japanese families on the West Coast of the United States lost everything.
They were sent to desert prisons.
Yama and Teruko's tiny New York City apartment overflowed with family, escaping.

The FBI said, "You are Japanese, suspicious."

The police said, "You are Japanese, show us your identification."

The neighbors said, "You are Japanese, you could be a spy."

I was born in Seattle. I am building my life, just like you.

Every bitter sound made a brick.

Each brick built a stronger foundation.

He added lines.

He didn't want to feel the way they were trying to make him feel.

He made shapes.

He brought in light.

He had a family, a Japanese American family,
that needed a place to live.
First, they were turned away. Again and again.
But then . . .

. . . they found a home.
An old farmhouse in a town without
red lines and cruel rules.
They built and they grew.

At his office, Yama worked and wondered.
How can I make a space of light with a feeling of open doors?
And air that breathes, "Everyone is welcome here"?
Shapes combined with lines combined with nature's light.

Serenity. Surprise. Delight.

Yama became his own boss. Signed his own drawings.
Made buildings where people worked in harmony.
Where people worked in peace.
For many years, he worked long, hard hours.
Too long, too hard. He worked until his body said, *Rest now*.

So he traveled and marveled.
Soar, said the quiet voice inside as his spirit
lifted into the arcs of the Alhambra.

Peace like this, it said as he beheld sun glinting on still water and paths of smooth round stones at the Katsura Palace.

Inspired, Yama returned to fill his office with big thinkers from around the world. Architects who worked side by side. People from many countries called Yama, asking him to design their buildings. The spaces he built connected to the humanity of everyday people.

Work places, learning spaces, travel hubs, and sacred spots to gather were filled with—

serenity, surprise, and delight.

His work grew, his name grew. The pressure upon him, that grew too.
He made mistakes and had regrets that would take time to fully understand.
People he worked with didn't always agree or share his vision.
Things didn't always work out the way he planned.

But so often, Yama found his way.
Bringing the outside world in.
Letting the sun shine through ceilings.
Illuminating shapes.
The reflecting water of a still pool
quieting a busy mind.
So one might sit, in peace.

His shapes, lines, and light
brought to so many
serenity, surprise, and delight.

And there was home.
A home he made of shapes and lines and light.
A home filled with Teruko's music.
A home that was filled with children and then grandchildren.

Many years later, a terrible thing happened.

But he had died years before.

If he had been alive, his heart would have broken into one million pieces.

Not for the buildings, but for all the people who went to work there in peace.

For all their families.

And for what happened afterward.

I lived there, then, in New York City, and it made me wonder,
What do buildings stand upon?

There is the earth, the soil, the concrete, the steel beams. . . .
There are our stories . . .

And the feeling we have,
in that space that is made
from shapes,
    and lines,
        and light.

Dhahran Air Terminal; Dhahran, Saudi Arabia

**Northwestern National Life Insurance Company;
Minneapolis, Minnesota**

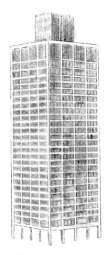

Michigan Consolidated Gas Company; Detroit, Michigan

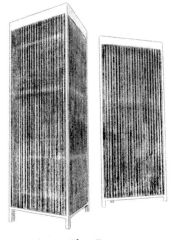

**Century Plaza Towers;
Century City, Los Angeles, California**

AUTHOR'S NOTE

It is hard to fit an entire life into the pages of a picture book. My grandfather had a big life, full of profound challenges, stunning achievements, and everyday moments. Born to immigrants, he grew up in a country that didn't trust him, didn't have space for him, didn't see him. He decided to change that. He would make space. He would be seen.

Minoru Yamasaki was born December 1, 1912, in Nihomachi, Seattle's bustling Japantown. He described his first home, a precariously perched tenement in the Yesler Hill section, as "apt to slide down the slope to the street below" at any moment. The family had only cold water and an outhouse out back. Although the conditions were primitive, he remembered that period of his life, surrounded by a vibrant community of other industrious, creative Japanese and Japanese Americans, as a time of fun and adventure.

Outside was another world. Minoru and his friends were not allowed to swim in the public swimming pools (except at the YMCA) and were relegated to watching movies from the upper balconies, even when the entire theater down below remained empty.

Minoru's father, Tsunejiro (John), worked multiple jobs throughout Minoru's childhood, stocking shoes on weekdays and cleaning the floors of a chocolate factory on weekends, which enabled the family to move into better housing. In school, Minoru was at the top of his class, without knowing what path he would follow—until a visit from his Uncle Koken, who had graduated with a degree in architecture from the University of California and was headed to Chicago to begin his first job. It was during that visit that he unrolled some drawings and Minoru "almost exploded with excitement."

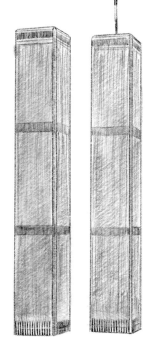

**World Trade Center;
New York, New York**

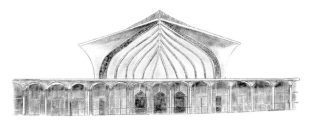

North Shore Congregation Israel; Glencoe, Illinois

Michigan State Medical Society Building; East Lansing, Michigan

From that moment on, he knew he would become an architect.

Minoru studied architecture at the University of Washington under Lionel Pries, who encouraged him even during times when he didn't know if the career was the right choice. To pay for school, Minoru, and his brother, Ken, after him, worked in the salmon canneries of Alaska—one of the few places that would hire young Nisei men. The conditions he described there were dehumanizing: physically dangerous, filthy, infested, and exploitative.

Minoru graduated with one of the best grade records in the history of the architecture school. Prior to the year of his graduation, the school had always awarded the top students a scholarship to study at the Society of Beaux Arts in Paris, but that year it canceled the scholarship so as not to grant it to Minoru. Greatly upset by this act, Tsuenjiro took the family on a trip to Japan that they could barely afford. The architecture and aesthetic of Japan impacted Minoru greatly. The exchange between the natural world and human-made structures remained with him and became a foundational principle in his own work.

Minoru moved to New York City in 1934. It was the Great Depression. Anti-Asian sentiment was high. No one was hiring architects, much less Japanese American architects from a public university. Eventually, he was brought on to a team to help make drawings for a competition. The firm won the competition and hired Minoru, thus beginning his career as a full-time architect. Soon after, the United States entered World War II, and after moving to a different firm, Minoru was assigned to design the Sampson Naval Station in upstate New York. Despite having been thoroughly investigated by the FBI, the army, and the navy, he still recalled being turned away at the gate by military police who saw him as a security threat.

Temple Beth-El; Bloomfield Township, Michigan

Founder's Hall, Shinji Shumeikai; Shiga Prefecture, Japan

Federal Science Pavilion, Seattle World's Fair; Seattle, Washington

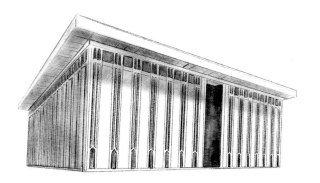

Saudi Arabian Monetary Agency Head Office; Riyadh, Saudi Arabia

Olin Hall, Carleton College; Northfield, Minnesota

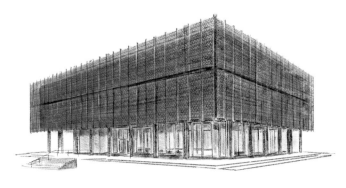

Reynolds Metals Regional Sales Office; Southfield, Michigan

St. Louis Lambert Airport Terminal; St. Louis, Missouri

On December 5, 1941, Minoru married my grandmother, Teruko, who was on a full scholarship at the Juilliard School of music to become a concert pianist. Two nights after their wedding, on the night of the attack on Pearl Harbor, Teruko's father, Anko, was arrested and sent to a military prison, having been deemed dangerous because he was part-owner of a produce market. Because their family business was lost in one instant and their home in the next, Teruko, her sister, Aki, and her brother, Jimmy, all had to drop out of school. Aki, Jimmy, and their mother, Toshi, were sent to a "camp" in Colorado. Minoru's parents, with the help of Minoru's bosses at the architecture firm, were able to escape Seattle and travel to New York City, narrowly avoiding the mass incarceration of over 120,000 Japanese and Japanese Americans from the West Coast for the duration of World War II.

Teruko and Minoru spent the years of the war in their one-bedroom apartment on the Upper East Side of Manhattan, with Minoru's parents and brother, Ken. It was a brutal time to be Japanese in the United States, but they were supported by Minoru's architecture firm and treated well by their landlord, who never raised their rent or met them with anything other than kindness as their tiny apartment overflowed with family, escaping.

After the war, Minoru worked at various architecture firms and eventually found himself in Detroit. He was respected and well-paid but he was prohibited from buying a home in what were considered the city's best suburbs because he was Japanese. He, Teruko, and his parents settled on an old farmhouse in Troy, Michigan, where they raised my Aunt Carol, Uncle Taro, and my father, Kim.

When Minoru created his own office, Yamasaki and Associates, in 1959, he was determined to hire

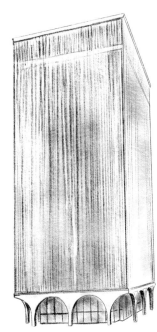

IBM Office building; Seattle, Washington

the best architects from around the world and create a vibrant, healthy work environment where the brightest minds could do their best work. When, years later, he won the commission to design the World Trade Center, all of a sudden he had to grow his small office to accommodate the demands of the project. The responsibility of being an employer to a much larger staff wasn't anything he took lightly. He was steadfast in his devotion to his employees, who returned that loyalty in the work they did for the firm.

Minoru was consumed by the idea of making buildings that created feelings of uplift and what he described as *serenity, surprise, and delight.* At that time, trends in architecture were to use new technology to overwhelm, intimidate, or amaze. Minoru wanted to use shapes and structures at a human scale that created a feeling of peace. He was interested in how the new technology could work with what we knew from architectural traditions of the past. He especially drew inspiration from forms found in nature, Islamic architecture, the great cathedrals of Europe, and in the interplay between buildings and the natural world found in the traditional architecture of Japan.

Although highly successful by any measure, Minoru was sometimes harshly criticized by the architecture world. Reviews of his buildings that could only be described as racist would start out by talking about his body—his small frame—and his decorative approach to his buildings. He would describe the emotional experience of a space and the shapes and light that can achieve that; and critics would call him frivolous. Reading those reviews was painful for him and took its toll over time. In the context of the anti-Japanese hostilities during his lifetime, I often find it hard to separate some critiques of his work from the fact that he was a Japanese American man who did not come from the privileged, white world of the architecture establishment.

It was a surprise for me to learn that my grandfather's work was not often taught in architecture schools and that he was mostly known for the World

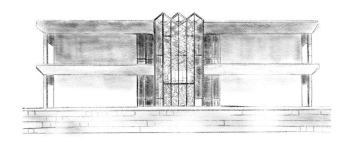

McGregor Memorial Community Conference Center, Wayne State University; Detroit, Michigan

DeRoy Auditorium, Wayne State University; Detroit, Michigan

Northminster Presbyterian Church; Troy, Michigan

Ranier Tower; Seattle, Washington

**Royce Chapel, U.S. Naval Training Station, Sampson;
Lake Seneca, New York**

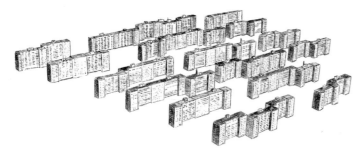

Pruitt-Igoe; St. Louis, Missouri

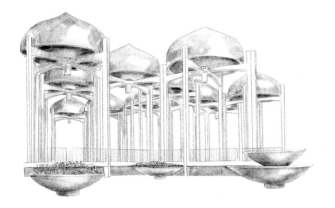

U.S. Pavilion, World Agricultural Fair; New Delhi, India

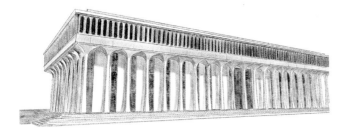

Robertson Hall, Princeton University; Princeton, New Jersey

Trade Center and for the terribly troubled and complex public housing experiment, the Pruitt-Igoe apartments in St. Louis, Missouri. It seemed wrong that someone with such a legacy could be known primarily for the two projects that least represented who he was as a human being and as an architect. I also knew how esteemed he was in the Japanese American community and how he was seen as a symbol of hope and success for so many who had lost everything during World War II. To this day, Japanese American elders tell me how much Grandpa has meant to them and their families and I know that his role in the community was not something he took lightly.

I have wanted to write this story for a long time. When I was growing up, I didn't want to become an artist because I felt the pressure to do something great, like my grandfather, or be able to play the piano like my grandmother, or win the Pulitzer Prize like my Uncle Taro—it was too much. But as I got older, I realized that what I loved were stories, and finding ways to tell stories that don't often get told—stories that help us shine a light on something that we all need to see a little more clearly. Grandpa always told my dad that drawing was simply looking carefully; truly seeing something. This book is my attempt to draw the story of his life and work, to take the time to see him a little more clearly.

Yamasaki family residence; Bloomfield Hills, Michigan

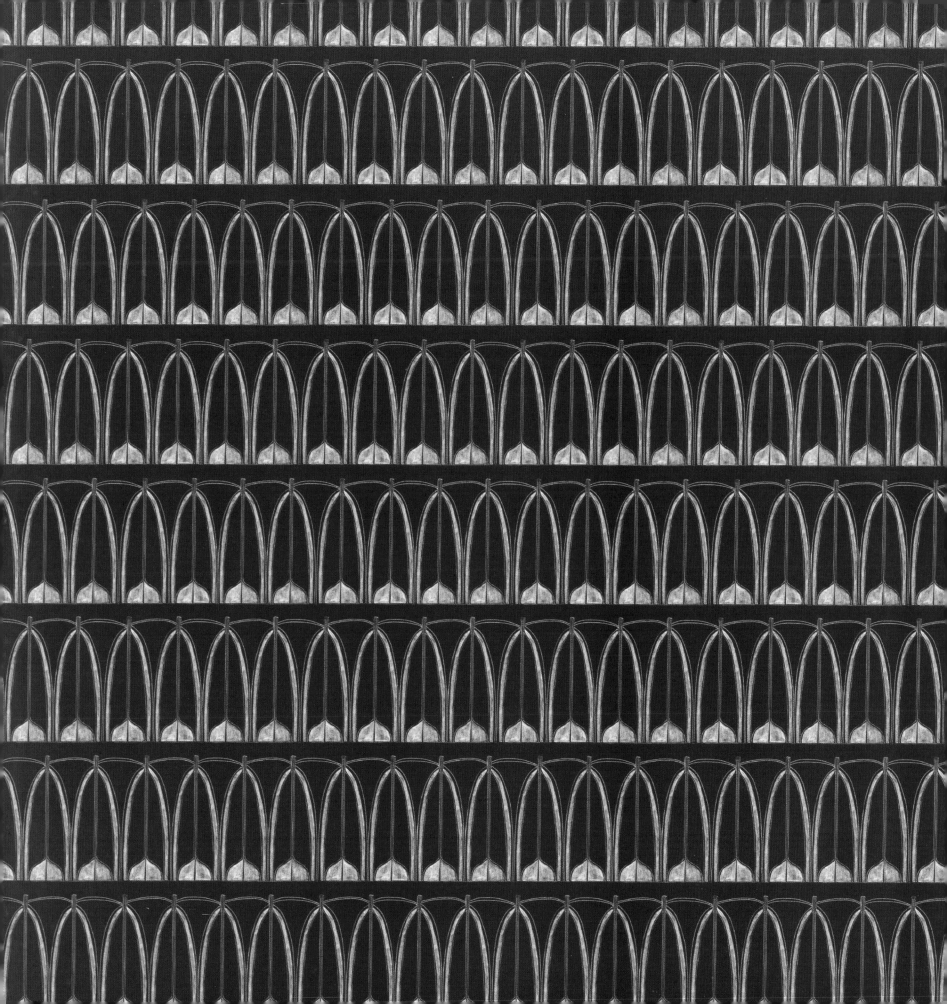